BE A MAKER!

Maker Projects for Kids Who Love
PRINTMAKING

JOAN MARIE GALAT

Crabtree Publishing Company
www.crabtreebooks.com

Crabtree Publishing Company

www.crabtreebooks.com

Author: Joan Marie Galat

Series Research and Development: Reagan Miller

Editors: Sarah Eason, and Philip Gebhardt

Proofreader: Wendy Scavuzzo

Editorial director: Kathy Middleton

Design: Paul Myerscough

Layout: Keith Williams

Cover design: Paul Myerscough

Photo research: Rachel Blount

**Production coordinator and
    prepress technician:** Tammy McGarr

Print coordinator: Margaret Amy Salter

Consultant: Jennifer Turliuk, CEO MakerKids

Production coordinated by Calcium Creative

Photo Credits:

t=Top, bl=Bottom Left, br=Bottom Right

Paul Bartlett RBSA, Senior RBA: p. 25; Christine Bradshaw: p. 23; Anne Crews: p. 9; Lumi/Brittany Rouse: p. 20; Shutterstock: 13Smile: p. 8; Dimitris K: p. 26; Julia Karo: p. 27; Val Lawless: p. 4; Petr Lerch: p. 18; Lunatictm: p. 5; Marcovarro: p. 19; Mr&Mrs Marcha: p. 24; Rosstek: p. 7; Betty Shelton: p. 22; Vectorfusionart: p. 21; Tudor Photography: pp. 10–11, 16–17, 28–29; Wikimedia Commons: Lionel Allorge: pp. 1, 15; Unknown Japanese copyists after Katsushika Hokusai: p. 6; Toni Pecoraro: p. 14; Zephyris: pp. 12, 13.

Cover: Tudor Photography.

For Jessica, a dear and inspiring maker

Library and Archives Canada Cataloguing in Publication

Galat, Joan Marie, 1963-, author
        Maker projects for kids who love printmaking /
Joan Marie Galat.

(Be a maker!)
Includes index.
Issued in print and electronic formats.
ISBN 978-0-7787-2889-4 (hardcover).--
ISBN 978-0-7787-2902-0 (softcover).--
ISBN 978-1-4271-1912-4 (HTML)

        1. Prints--Technique--Juvenile literature. I. Title. II. Series: Be a maker!

NE860.G35 2017   j769   C2016-907380-7
                                      C2016-907381-5

Library of Congress Cataloging-in-Publication Data

Names: Galat, Joan Marie, 1963- author.
Title: Maker projects for kids who love printmaking /
    Joan Marie Galat.
Description: New York : Crabtree Publishing Company, 2017. |
    Series: Be a maker! | Includes index. | Audience: Ages 10-14+. |
    Audience: Grades 4 to 6.
Identifiers: LCCN 2016050632 (print) | LCCN 2016052295 (ebook)
    ISBN 9780778728894 (reinforced library binding) |
    ISBN 9780778729020 (pbk.) |
    ISBN 9781427119124 (Electronic HTML)
Subjects: LCSH: Prints--Technique--Juvenile literature.
Classification: LCC NE860 .G35 2017 (print) | LCC NE860 (ebook)
    | DDC 769--dc23
LC record available at https://lccn.loc.gov/2016050632

Crabtree Publishing Company
www.crabtreebooks.com   1-800-387-7650

Printed in Canada/022017/CH20161214

Published in Canada
Crabtree Publishing
616 Welland Ave.
St. Catharines, Ontario
L2M 5V6

Published in the United States
Crabtree Publishing
PMB 59051
350 Fifth Avenue, 59th Floor
New York, New York 10118

Published in the United Kingdom
Crabtree Publishing
Maritime House
Basin Road North, Hove
BN41 1WR

Published in Australia
Crabtree Publishing
3 Charles Street
Coburg North
VIC, 3058

CONTENTS

MAKE AN IMPRESSION!

From pictures to patterns, art made by printmaking—the process of transferring an image from one surface to another—is all around. Your T-shirt might feature a funky **silk-screen** design. Framed **prints** may hang in your home or school. Digital prints appear on cakes, paper cups, and billboards. Present-day art looks new yet may be produced using methods that are thousands of years old.

WHAT IS PRINTMAKING?

Traditional printmaking forms include **relief**, silk screen, **lithography**, and **intaglio** (in-TAL-yoh). Artists use these methods and newer techniques to create stunning **original** art. Through these processes, multiple prints of an image can be made. Because each print is individually created by hand, it is an original work rather than a **reproduction**, or exact copy. For example, if you dip your thumb in ink, then press it on paper, it creates a print. Repeating the process yields another print. Although they look similar, the two thumbprints are each unique works.

PRINTMAKERS

It is in the word itself—printmakers are makers! Printmakers may print on cloth, clay, paper, or **ceramics**. They develop new tools and fresh methods, and take advantage of computer technology. Digital art gives artists even more options, but traditional printmaking is still popular. Classic techniques, practiced over hundreds of years, provide makers with a place to begin, learn, and build their skills.

Images are made up of both positive and negative areas. The raised star on this potato stamp creates **positive space** when it is printed on paper, while the cutaway area leaves **negative space**.

TIME TO MAKE!

Why be a maker? It is fun to dream up an idea and take on a challenge, knowing anything might happen. Sometimes things turn out as expected, but not always. Surprises are part of the process—and a big part of the fun! A **makerspace** is a great place to get started. Often housed in schools or libraries, these spaces provide makers with ideas, materials, and tools. You might find a **three-dimensional** (3-D) printer, a printing press, design software, or other specialized equipment there.

A silk-screen print can appear 3-D. It can be hard to tell whether a picture was made with a paintbrush or by pressing paint through a screen.

Be a Maker!

A makerspace can be as small as a toolbox or as large as a workshop. Make your own go-to makerspace—a box of tools and materials that you can you use to make prints. What will you add? Paper? Paintbrushes? A brayer? Be creative!

5

HISTORY OF PRINTMAKING

Can you imagine seeing pictures only once or twice a year, or perhaps never at all? Before printmaking evolved, all art was original. You would never see an artistic creation unless you visited a church or the home of a wealthy person. Printmaking brought this beauty to everyday people.

BUILDING BLOCKS

Artists liked the idea of more people being able to view and buy their work! The first prints were made by carving a picture into wood. This created a printing surface called a relief. The image was coated in ink and pressed onto cloth to make multiple prints. During the 1700s in Japan, an art form called ukiyo-e (YOO-key-oh AY) became popular. Meaning "pictures of the floating world," ukiyo-e first illustrated city life in Edo (now Tokyo), and was later applied to landscapes. Printmakers used multiple blocks and colors to create intricate prints, making separate designs and blocks for different parts of an image. Because they used water-based paints, it took perfect timing to achieve the desired tones before the paint dried. Four people—a designer, **engraver**, printer, and publisher—worked together. The process was labor-intensive, but the results were precise and elegant.

This famous Japanese print called *Under the Wave off Kanagawa* shows a wave about to crash into a boat. An artist named Hokusai designed the image, then a master carver carved the woodblocks used to make the print.

Movable type is a printing method in which blocks of individual letters can be arranged to make any word.

FOR THE MASSES

Printmaking came to everyday people around 1390, when paper became inexpensive enough to allow mass production. Playing cards and devotional images became affordable and popular. More people could enjoy art, but that was not the only change. Ideas and knowledge spread more easily, especially as improved methods of printing and papermaking evolved. Images that shared information about science, geography, and architecture helped these fields progress. Historical images provided a record of the past. When Johannes Gutenberg invented the printing press in the mid-1400s, movable type made it possible to spread information, along with **woodcut** illustrations, even more quickly. Today, libraries and the Internet allow people around the world to access knowledge shared through printmaking. It is no longer necessary to be rich to access art and knowledge.

Be a Maker!

You do not have to go far to find printmaking examples. Observe your surroundings. How many kinds of printed materials can you spot right now?

FROM IDEA TO PRINT

Printmaking sounds like a mechanical process, but it is really the art of transferring ink, usually by hand, from one surface to another. The printmaker's choice of tools, materials, and methods determine how the finished product will look.

PLANNING A PRINT

Printmaking takes patience and time. Before you start preparing your **plate** or **stencil**, think about the **composition** of your print. Will you create a pattern? Do you want to create a symmetrical look, so that the shape and position of your design are balanced across the printed area? Or would you prefer an abstract appearance in which your print represents an object, but does not actually look like that object? Consider whether color is needed, and how you will arrange lines or textured areas to create your vision.

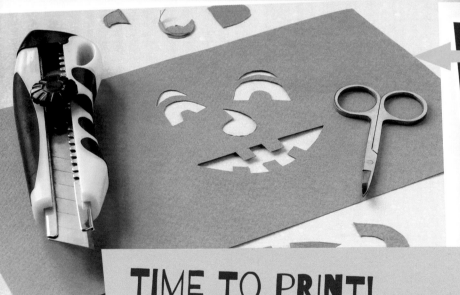

When making a stencil, use scrap paper to practice cutting the design.

TIME TO PRINT!

Printmaking begins with sketching an image, picking a material to print, and selecting a surface on which to transfer the image. The design must be drawn, **etched**, or carved into a master plate, or made into a stencil. A brayer or **dauber** is used to apply ink or paint to the plate or stencil. A print is "pulled" by pressing the paper to the plate or forcing paint through a stencil.

PRACTICE MAKES PERFECT

Prints do not always turn out to the artist's liking right away. An artist might ink up a plate to see how the image looks, then make changes until he or she is happy with the print. Artists often number their final prints to show how many were made. The numeral appears as a fraction, such as 10/30—indicating the tenth print of the 30 created. The plates used to make the prints may be destroyed to create more valuable, **limited edition** prints.

MAKE YOUR MARK

Many printmakers do not sign their full name on a print. Instead, they use a **monogram** of their initials, which is sometimes accompanied by a symbol. The monogram is often carved into the plate itself. Other times, an artist signs the finished print, usually in pencil.

Cats   Anne Irby Chaus

Printmakers must choose durable materials if they want to pull several prints from a plate. This vinyl-cut relief *Cats in Clover* was pulled 45 times.

Be a Maker!

How do the tools and materials an artist uses help to make a work unique? Why might a printmaker choose one method over another?

MAKE IT!
GELATIN PLATE PRINT

A **monotype** is a single, unique print pulled from a plate. Make your own **gelatin** plate, then create a one-of-a-kind print using found objects from around the house or in the great outdoors.

1

- With an adult's help, carefully pour 2½ cups (20 oz) of boiling water into the glass measuring cup.
- Add the packets of gelatin, one at a time. Stir with your spatula until the mixture is smooth.
- Strain the mixture into one of your bowls, then strain it back into the measuring cup. This should remove any remaining lumps.

2

- Next, add the glycerin to the mixture. Stir well with your spoon.
- Line your pan with plastic wrap, then pour in the mixture.
- Smooth over with your icing knife.
- Put the pan in your refrigerator.
- Leave for two days to cure (the gelatin mixture will set solid), then remove from the refrigerator.

3

- Cover a work surface with newspaper.
- Roll a roller in paint. Cover the plate with paint using smooth, even strokes.

10

- Arrange the items on the painted plate.
- Then place a sheet of paper over the plate.

4

5

- Use the second roller to firmly press the paper onto the plate to create your print.
- Peel back the paper.
- When you are done making prints, gently clean the plate and your tools with soap and water. Store it in the refrigerator for up to two weeks.

Make It Even Better!

How does your art appear on patterned paper or newsprint? What about on a different material, such as a handkerchief or pillowcase? What happens if you use other types of paint? How can you rearrange your items to tell a story?

CONCLUSION

Artists make new creations by playing with tools, materials, and techniques. Working with your hands inspires new ideas. Printmakers soon realize that adding or taking away elements can create a whole new look. It is fun to practice and experiment!

STAMP IT!

Relief printing is the process of printing a raised surface. Picture a rubber stamp's protruding ridges. In printmaking, the unwanted parts of a surface material are cut or etched away. This creates a blank background and a raised image, called a relief. Ink is applied to the image to pull a print.

TOOLS OF THE TRADE

Artists making reliefs traditionally use woodblocks or **linoleum** tiles as plates. Knives and chiseling tools are used to cut the design. A tool called a brayer is rolled across the plate to spread ink over the raised areas.

Strong and light, high-quality plywood provides a flat, smooth surface for etching. Some artists use a wire brush to enhance the wood's natural grain. Others sand the wood to hide it!

MATERIALS

A woodblock artist begins with a design, then chooses materials that will best illustrate that design. Selecting the right wood is important. Softwoods are easier to cut, while hardwoods hold greater detail. Plywood splinters easily, but artists using plywood can create large prints that measure 4 by 8 feet (1.2 by 2.4 m)!

FROM IDEA TO ART

1 A picture is drawn in pencil on plain white paper. The picture may be scanned and manipulated on a computer.

2 The drawing is transferred to the plate by rubbing it onto the block, or by placing a printed picture on the block. The image is then inked with a pen to make the lines easier to see.

3 The material is cut using a knife or chisel, using careful, shallow strokes, away from the body.

4 Ink is applied to a brayer by first using a putty knife to spread ink onto a glass sheet. The brayer is rolled against the inked glass until it is evenly covered, then rolled across the plate.

5 A sheet of paper is placed on the inked plate, then pressed with a wide spoon. The paper is slowly lifted from the block and allowed to dry.

6 The artist evaluates the results, deciding whether more material needs to be cut away, or more or less ink should be used in the next printing.

This is the moment you have been working toward! When pulling your print, make sure your hands are free of ink and that you have a clean place to set down the finished product.

Be a Maker!

Printmakers need to think sideways and backwards. Relief images appear horizontally flipped when printed. Cut-away parts create white spaces rather than inked areas. An easy way to make a reference is to write a word on a piece of scrap paper, then hold it up to a mirror to make sure it reads correctly. With a parent's permission, you can also search "mirror text generator" online to flip letters and words.

ETCH IT AND DRAW IT!

Printmakers can choose from many techniques. They might use intaglio to engrave a print from an image created below a plate's surface. Lithography reproduces an image drawn on a surface.

PRESSING IN

The word *intaglio* means "to cut" in Italian. Intaglio is the opposite of relief. Using tools such as needles, chisels, and **burins**, a printmaker marks an image into a metal plate. When using the etching method, acidic chemicals are applied to burn away parts of the plate. Ink is then spread across the plate. A dauber is used to push ink into the grooves. The extra ink is wiped off, leaving ink in the cut areas only. A piece of paper is placed on the plate, then covered by a blanket or other material. Rollers apply pressure that pushes the paper into the grooves. The ink is absorbed, leaving behind a raised, reverse impression of the original image.

Each tool helps an artist achieve a different tone or texture. Some are better for blurring lines, while others are more suited to creating sharp grooves.

DRAWING ON

The lithograph technique allows artists to retain the detailed characteristics of a drawing. An image is sketched directly onto a plate or flat stone using a greasy crayon, or ink called **tusche**. After the image is complete, water is used to make the surface of the plate damp. Then ink is applied. The ink sticks to the greasy marks, but not to the wet areas. Paper is pressed against the surface to absorb the ink and pull a print. Lithographic printing allows for more color tones by applying more or less water to create an effect similar to the sketch. Color can be added by hand or with separate plates.

The ink from a brayer only sticks to the greased image in a lithographic print.

Be a Maker!

You do not need fancy equipment to try out many of the different printmaking techniques. Makers have found innovative ways to use household items to craft original works of art, such as using white vinegar and vegetable oil to make lithographic prints. With an adult's permission, research alternate printing processes online and try them yourself!

MAKE IT!
LEAF RELIEF

You can make an interesting relief with materials found in nature. Make a leaf relief to capture and enjoy the beauty of the outdoors year-round.

1
- Spread the newspaper on a table or other work surface to catch any paint drips.
- Place your recycled paper on the surface, then place your leaves vein-side-up on the newspaper. Position the leaves to create an interesting arrangement.
- Take a photograph of it.

- Paint the entire veined side of each leaf.

2

16

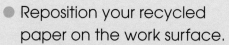

- Reposition your recycled paper on the work surface.
- Place each leaf paint-side down onto the recycled paper in the arrangement you planned. (Check against the photo you took in step 1 to make sure you have them in the right position.)
- Gently press the leaves onto the paper. Then carefully remove them one by one.

3

4

- Your leaf relief is complete!

CONCLUSION

Relief printing can be achieved in two ways: by cutting away materials, or building up materials to make a design stand out. Leaf veins are natural reliefs. Nothing needs to be removed or added to give the impression of depth. How well did positive and negative spaces create depth in your leaf art? What other natural materials could you find in nature to create interesting prints?

Make It Even Better!

See what happens when you make overlapping images. Try rearranging your leaves to form animal shapes. Experiment with colors to see if your creation becomes more interesting or simply distracting. Why do some plant species make more distinct reliefs?

17

SCREEN IT!

Silk screening can be used to transfer images to almost any surface. Think paper, cloth, metal, wood, clay, or plastic! The process creates lines that are sharper than the lines in block printing. It is one of the easiest methods for making a multicolored print. **Serigraphy**, another name for silk screening, comes from *seri*, the Latin word for silk, and *graphos*—Greek for "to draw or write." The technique is also called silk printing or screen printing, since silk is no longer the most commonly used material.

SCREEN PRINTING

Screen printing makes use of a rectangular frame, tightly covered in silk, polyester, or another fine fabric. A stencil provides a barrier that ensures ink reaches only the areas to be printed. When designing, the artist must consider positive space, which allows ink to pass though the screen, and negative space, which remains blank.

Printmakers position the stencil underneath the screen in the center. Separate screens are used for each color.

FROM STENCIL TO T-SHIRT

1 The artist creates a design, then uses a laser printer to print the image on a **transparency**. Another method uses **photographic emulsion** to transfer the image.

2 Using a knife, the image is cut to create a stencil.

3 The artist positions the stencil on the T-shirt, then places the silk (or polyester) screen on top of the stencil.

4 Ink is pushed through the screen with a **squeegee**. The stencil stops ink from touching the areas meant to remain unprinted. If multiple colors are required, the process is repeated with another screen and ink color.

Makers and Shakers

Andy Warhol

Not everyone gets inspired by a soup can, but Andy Warhol (1928–1987) was a printmaker with new ideas. He painted 32 Campbell's Soup cans onto canvases in 1962, hand stamping the pattern along the bottom of each can. In 1964, Warhol began silk screening soup cans onto shopping bags. He also experimented with screening photographs and tried to make his original prints look mass-produced, like advertising images. Using a photo of movie icon Marilyn Monroe, Warhol created prints of the same picture in different colors. His style revolutionized the screen print in America.

Warhol explored a new way of expressing creativity by turning an everyday object into art. His inspiration came from eating Campbell's Soup for lunch every day for 20 years!

A MODERN TWIST

Printmakers take advantage of technological advances to create new kinds of prints.

PICTURE PERFECT

When photography became possible, makers began to combine elements of photography and etching. They developed **photogravure**—a technique in which a design on a transparency is placed onto a chemically treated zinc or copper plate. When the plate is exposed to ultraviolet light, the design transfers to the plate, which can then be etched and inked for printing.

Makers and Shakers

Jesse Genet

Jesse Genet (born 1987) began building her printmaking business in high school. She wanted to create photography that people could touch. However, she could not get the printing results she wanted. One day, while developing photographs, she envisioned a solution that would use sunlight, a **negative**, and a light-sensitive fabric dye. Along with a partner from design school, she created Inkodye, a chemical that allows printing on fabric, and a process called Lumi for making one-of-a-kind prints using sunlight. Wanting to show others how to design prints without expensive equipment, they created an app for working with designs and built an online community where people can share their projects.

Genet was inspired to start Lumi by her love of fashion, photography, technology, and printing.

GOING DIGITAL

Today's technology allows further innovation. Printmakers can draw on a tablet to digitize original sketches, or use a scanner to input images into a computer. Artists can create and modify art with a computer before starting a hands-on printing process. Software makes it possible for makers to save an original print, then experiment with a wide variety of options. Colors might be changed or images rotated, **elongated**, and repeated. This flexibility makes it even easier for creators to design art that can be printed in multiple ways—on T-shirts, rubber, glass, canvas, or other surfaces.

With an adult's permission, check out some of the software and apps available that combine printmaking and technology.

PRINTMAKING 2.0

Apps offer artists even more ways to play with design. Makers can perfect their skills in a virtual manner, instead of using physical materials and tools to learn techniques. Software can make it faster and easier to experiment with the composition and colors of an image. An app is a less-costly design tool that offers multiple chances to try out new ideas.

PRESENT YOUR PRINTS

The prints are dry and tools stored, yet there is still work to do! Printmakers often take on the roles of record keeper and salesperson, too. Each print in an **edition** must be numbered and recorded. Prints are photographed to create a digital portfolio, allowing artists to showcase their best work. Finally, printmakers must consider the best way to present their work. Prints may be shown in an art gallery, as well as displayed or sold online.

FRAMED!

Once you have created art, the next step is finding the best way to show it off. The right frame can help make a print the center of attention. Frames may be made of wood or metal, and can contain intricate detail or be smooth and plain. **Mats** are used to prevent prints from sticking to glass, as well as to draw the eye toward the image. It is important to make sure the frame does not distract the viewer from the art it holds. Finally, a printmaker must decide how to display prints on a wall. Some images shine best alone; others can form beautiful groupings.

Mats come in all shapes and sizes. Choose a style that best showcases your work.

This windmill image was made using a technique that takes careful planning: reduction printing. One block is used to print the base color, then the block is "reduced" by carving away more material to apply the next color. The process can be repeated multiple times.

YOU BE THE JUDGE!

An original print sounds like a one-of-a-kind piece of art, but an original is not wholly unique. Though each impression is slightly different, each print is part of a "set of originals." A benefit of printmaking is that it allows more people to view the same image and explore the parts of a print. Each viewer takes away different impressions. One person may focus on capturing a lifelike image, while another senses a mood, relationship, or story within a print. Talking about these impressions can lead to artistic **collaborations**. Printmakers and printers may work together to create art neither person could produce independently.

Be a Maker!

Think about ways to present your art without using a traditional frame. How might you present your print on a bookstand, plate holder, or grooved ledge? How might a mat add to your print's visual appeal? In what other ways could you display your art?

PLAYING WITH PRINTMAKING

Most artists spend years developing a distinct style. Makers can improve their skills by making creativity a habit.

GET INSPIRED

Activities such as sketching, visiting galleries, or reading illustrated books can trigger inspiration. Studying realistic images helps printmakers create more lifelike designs. Experimenting with other forms of art boosts innovation. Collaborating provides the opportunity to share, critique, and grow. Experienced printmakers know that playing with art to see where an idea leads is part of the artistic process.

STAY INSPIRED

The maker attitude accepts that things go wrong. Ink will smudge, paint will drip, tools will break. Printmakers would soon be bored if every print turned out perfectly. True satisfaction comes from overcoming difficulties, and improving though your own efforts. The best way to get past disappointment is to figure out what went wrong, so you can prevent a repeat incident. Remember—no one gets through life without problems. Think of a situation in which something goes wrong. How could it turn into a good thing?

Sometimes ideas only come once you pick up your tools and get started. It is fun to discover all the ways to be a maker.

INSPIRE OTHERS

Finding like-minded makers can double the fun! Working with another person to create a print will expose you to fresh ways of tackling challenges, and keep you from falling into the habit of always approaching art the same way. You might start a printmaking club with weekly or monthly get-togethers to make art, visit a gallery, or watch do-it-yourself videos to learn new techniques. Club activities could include making scrapbooks of reference images, or literally "printing" a newsletter about printmaking! You might even produce your own maker videos to share your projects and inspire others.

Printmaking techniques are combined in original ways to make prints. This printmaker used leaves to create rich textured trees. What materials or places will inspire your next print?

Makers and Shakers

Ellen Vaughan Kirk Grayson

Have you ever drawn a sketch to make sure you remember something that grabs your attention? Ellen Vaughan Kirk Grayson (1894–1995) was a printmaker who was fond of making sketches. She loved the Rocky Mountains and sketched to remember how the light looked at a particular moment, or how colors, textures, and images might work together in a print. Printmaking provided a way for her to share how she felt about the landscapes she loved.

PRINTMAKING WITH A MESSAGE

It is fun to be a maker, but can it also be important? Yes!
A maker's ability to communicate through art is invaluable.
It is only limited by imagination!

FUNCTIONAL ART

A print can spark emotions or raise issues that might not otherwise be shared. Just as a song can trigger a memory, a print can remind its audience of an actual place. It may highlight a period in history, or a startling new idea. Prints can influence viewers far beyond the walls of a house or an art gallery. They can be used to adorn something most people exchange with one another—greeting cards! Art that serves a practical purpose, in addition to its visual appeal and ability to trigger emotion, is called functional art. You can see printmaking as functional art when original images are screened on cards, notebooks, clothing, bags, cushions, and other useful objects.

You probably have functional art in your closet or dresser. Take a closer look at the pictures and logos on your clothes, and consider what ideas the artists are trying to communicate.

MAKE IT YOUR OWN

Printmaking pairs well with other forms of art. How might a print look as a border around a painting or photograph? How can you use prints to enhance a school project? Think about creative ways you can express your personal interests through printmaking. What objects can you use as a stamp or a stencil? If you like sports, try using an old cleat as a stamp. For individuals who like fashion, silk screen one of your original designs on a hat, scarf, or T-shirt.

Display your prints with pride. Hang them at different levels to see what composition works best. Rearrange your groupings as you create new favorites.

Be a Maker!

Think of a symbol or word that shares a message. Sketch it on a piece of paper. When you are happy with the design, transfer your image onto a piece of thin cardboard. Cut it out to make a stencil. Be sure to leave a wide border around the image so it is easier to apply ink or paint through the cutouts.

MAKE IT!
SCREEN PRINT T-SHIRT

Bring out your favorite colors to screen print a T-shirt with an image that expresses your interests and personality. Use color and design to make a T-shirt that says, "This is me!"

YOU WILL NEED
- White T-shirt
- One embroidery hoop, ready to use
- White paper
- Sheet of contact paper
- Pencil
- Utility knife and cutting mat
- Nontoxic fabric paint
- A plastic card, such as a gift card
- One large plate

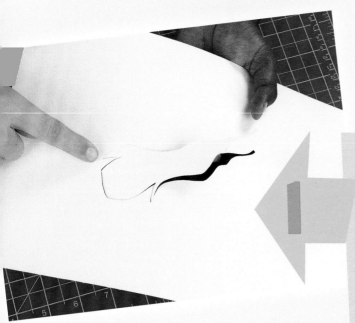

1
- Sketch your design on a sheet of plain white paper.
- When you are happy with your design, copy it onto the sheet of contact paper.
- Put the contact paper onto your cutting mat, and ask an adult to carefully cut out your design using the utility knife.

2
- Cut a circle around your design, so it will fit onto the embroidery hoop.
- Press the contact paper design to the center of your embroidery hoop—directly onto the fabric.

3
- Cover a work surface with newspaper.
- Put your T-shirt onto the newspaper.
- Lay a few sheets of newspaper beneath the top layer of your T-shirt to keep the paint from seeping through to the back of the T-shirt.

- Place the embroidery hoop in the center of the T-shirt. Ask a friend to hold the hoop in position.
- Pour some of your fabric paint onto a large plate.
- Scoop up a little of the paint with the plastic card.
- Carefully smooth the paint across the top of the contact paper design. Take care to run the paint smoothly and evenly across the design. You want the paint to evenly fill the area you have cut out as a stencil.

4

5

- Remove the embroidery hoop.
- Leave your T-shirt to dry overnight. Make sure it is fully dry before you wear it!

CONCLUSION

Art is all about exploring ideas and trying different approaches. It often stems from feelings that makers wish to express. Screen printing a T-shirt offers a method for showcasing original images, along with text. It is an effective way to communicate art as a message.

Make It Even Better!

Cut additional stencils to create a print arrangement or pattern that adds more visual interest to your design. How can you incorporate words to make your print stand out? How would your T-shirt look if you screened a sleeve, the back, or another area of the fabric?

GLOSSARY

brayer A handheld roller used for spreading ink evenly across a surface

burins Engraving tools used to cut V-shaped grooves into printing plates

ceramics Clay items that have been hardened by heating

collaborations Tasks in which two or more people work together

composition The placement of visual components in a work of art

dauber A tool used to spread ink on a screen or plate

edition All the copies of art that are printed at the same time

elongated Made longer

engraver A person who carves lines, letters, or designs into or onto a hard surface

etched To make a pattern using a chemical that cuts into metal or glass

gelatin A clear substance that is used to make jelly

innovative Introducing a new way to do something

intaglio The process of engraving or etching a metal plate

limited edition A fixed number of prints produced at the same time with the understanding that no other prints will be produced later

linoleum A thin, canvas-backed material used as a floor covering

lithography Printing from a surface that has been treated so ink only sticks to parts chosen by the artist

makerspace Where makers meet to share ideas, innovate, and invent

mats Flat materials, usually cardboard, used to create a border or space between a picture and frame

monogram A symbol made up of a person's initials

monotype A single print taken from a design painted or inked on a plate

negative An image in which light and dark areas are reversed

negative space The background of a picture

original Art that a printmaker has manually printed

photographic emulsion The light-sensitive coating on photographic film or paper

photogravure A printing process using a zinc or copper plate covered in a light-sensitive substance

plate The prepared surface a print is transferred from

positive space The main focus of a picture

prints Original art made by printmaking

relief An impression created by raised areas on a printing surface

serigraphy The fine art of screening prints onto paper

silk screen A printing process in which ink is forced through a stencil; also called a screen print

squeegee A rubber-edged blade used to spread a liquid across a surface

stencil A design cut from paper, plastic, or other materials to ensure that ink or paint only reaches areas to be printed

three-dimensional Appearing to have three dimensions (height, width, and depth)

transparency A clear plastic or film that light can shine through

tusche A greasy substance used for drawing on paper, stone, metal, or other surfaces

woodcut A printing method in which wood is carved away to create a raised surface to create a relief print

LEARNING MORE

BOOKS

Bautista, Traci. *Printmaking Unleashed: More Than 50 Techniques for Expressive Mark Making.* North Light Books, 2014.

Hanson, Anders. *Cool Printmaking: The Art of Creativity for Kids!* ABDO Publishing Company, 2009.

Meachen Rau, Dana. *Printmaking.* Cherry Lake Publishing, 2016.

Rhatigan, Joe, and Rain Newcomb. *Kids' Crafts: Stamp It!: 50 Amazing Projects to Make.* Lark Books, 2004.

WEBSITES

Try out some of the printmaking projects at DIY:
https://diy.org/skills/printmaker

Get crafty making solar prints using construction paper and the Sun:
www.instructables.com/id/DIY-Construction-Paper-Solar-Prints

Visit the Museum of Modern Art's website and explore examples of woodcuts, etching, lithography, and screen printing:
www.moma.org/interactives/projects/2001/whatisaprint/flash.html

Try your hand at creating floating chalk prints:
picklebums.com/floating-chalk-prints

Make a stencil with freezer paper:
www.stayathomeartist.com/2011/07/stencil-with-freezer-paper-harry-potter.html

INDEX

ABOUT THE AUTHOR

Joan Marie Galat is the author of more than a dozen books. She likes how the maker movement encourages innovation, problem solving, and idea sharing. Joan reminds makers that the creative process is meant to be as much fun as seeing a project completed.